W9-BTZ-010

MIKE TROUT

By Marie Morreale

REAL BIOS

Children's Press®
An Imprint of Scholastic Inc.

Photographs ©: cover: Rob Carr/Getty Images; back cover: Aaron Vincent Elkaim, The Canadian Press/AP Images; 1: Tom Donoghue/Newscom; 2, 3: Armando Arorizo/Newscom; 4-5: Erik Williams/Newscom; 6-7 background: Lisa Blumenfeld/Getty Images; 6 inset: Seth Poppel/Yearbook Library; 8: Deanne Fitzmaurice/Sports Illustrated/Getty Images; 9, 10: Seth Poppel/Yearbook Library; 11: Matt Brown/Getty Images; 12: Seth Poppel/Yearbook Library; 13: Jack Dempsey/AP Images; 14: Josh Thompson/Zuma Press; 15 top: Tribune Content Agency LLC/Alamy Images; 15 center: Joe Seer/Shutterstock, Inc.; 15 bottom: Drive Images/Alamy Images; 16: WENN Ltd/Alamy Images; 17 top: SlipFloat/Shutterstock, Inc.; 17 center top: James Steidl/Dreamstime; 17 center bottom: Ron Cortes/Newscom; 17 bottom: CaseyMartin/Shutterstock, Inc.; 18: Larry Goren/Four Seam Images; 21 top: Keith Birmingham/Zuma Press; 21 bottom: Larry Goren/Four Seam Images; 22: David Welker/Four Seam Images; 23 top: Keith Birmingham/Zuma Press; 23 bottom: Tony Dejak/AP Images; 24 top: Rob Carr/Getty Images; 24 bottom: Jonathan Daniel/Getty Images; 25: Kevin Sullivan/Newscom; 27: PN2 WENN Photos/Newscom; 28: Keith Birmingham/Zuma Press; 30: Bill Streicher/USA TODAY Sports; 31: Kirby Lee/Image of Sport/USA TODAY Sports; 32: Bill Streicher/USA TODAY Sports; 33: Peter Joneleit/Landov; 34: Joy R. Absalon/USA TODAY Sports; 35: Keith Birmingham/Zuma Press; 36: Tom Donoghue/Newscom; 36-41 background: conejota/Thinkstock; 36 blue paper and throughout: Nonnakrit/Shutterstock, Inc.; 36 pushpins and throughout: seregam/Thinkstock; 36 lined paper and throughout: My Life Graphic/Shutterstock, Inc.; 37 top left: Jonathan Moore/Getty Images; 37 top right: rvlsoft/Shutterstock, Inc.; 37 bottom left: Hong Vo/Shutterstock, Inc.; 37 bottom right: Keith Homan/Shutterstock, Inc.; 38: JStone/Shutterstock, Inc.; 39 top: Bill Florence/Shutterstock, Inc.; 39 bottom: Aspen Photo/Shutterstock, Inc.; 41 left: Juan DeLeon/Newscom; 41 right: Tom Donoghue/Newscom; 42: Joe Nicholson/USA TODAY Sports; 43, 45: Kevin Sullivan/Newscom.

Library of Congress Cataloging-in-Publication Data
Morreale, Marie.
 Mike Trout / by Marie Morreale.
    pages cm. — (Real bios)
 Includes bibliographical references and index.
 ISBN 978-0-531-22380-2 (library binding : alk. paper) —
 ISBN 978-0-531-22564-6 (paperback : alk. paper)
 1. Trout, Mike, 1991– —Juvenile literature. 2. Baseball play-
ers—United States—Biography—Juvenile literature. I. Title.
 GV865.T73M67 2016
 796.357092—dc23 [B]   2015026883

No part of this publication may be reproduced in whole or in part, or stored in a retrieval system, or transmitted in any form or by any means, electronic, mechanical, photocopying, recording, or otherwise, without written permission of the publisher. For information regarding permission, write to Scholastic Inc., Attention: Permissions Department, 557 Broadway, New York, NY 10012.

© 2016 Scholastic Inc.

All rights reserved. Published in 2016 by Children's Press, an imprint of Scholastic Inc.

Printed in the United States 113
SCHOLASTIC, CHILDREN'S PRESS, and associated logos are trademarks and/or registered trademarks of Scholastic Inc.

1 2 3 4 5 6 7 8 9 10 R 25 24 23 22 21 20 19 18 17 16

MEET MIKE!
BASEBALL SUPERSTAR!

Mike Trout plays center field for the Los Angeles Angels of Anaheim. He may only be in his midtwenties, but he's already been compared to baseball legends such as Mickey Mantle and Derek Jeter. But these comparisons aren't what brings a grin to Mike's boyish face. Home runs . . . **RBIs** . . . stolen bases . . . these are the things that make him happy. And don't forget about the future championships he dreams of winning!

When he's off the field, Mike is Mr. Casual, most comfortable in a T-shirt and jeans. If any World Series rings come along, they will probably go straight to his parents' house in Millville, New Jersey, and be displayed in his "man cave." If you want to know more about what makes Mike tick, read this *Real Bio*. You'll learn about his family life, his career, and more.

L.A. Angels' Mike is cheered— even at rival Dodger stadium!

CONTENTS

It's going, going, gone!
Another home run for Mike!

MIKE TROUT'S SWIM TO WIN

FROM MILLVILLE TO THE MAJOR LEAGUES

Michael Nelson Trout was born on August 7, 1991. He was a perfect addition to Debbie and Jeff Trout's young family, which also included Mike's older sister, Teal, and brother, Tyler. The family couldn't wait for baby Mikey to come home from the hospital.

Mike's parents were both educators. Jeff taught high school history and coached football and baseball. Debbie was a teaching assistant. Education was important in the Trout household, but baseball was right up there, too. In his younger days, Jeff had played second base at the University of Delaware. After college, he was

Even as a toddler, Mike was very athletic.

MIKE PLAYED ONE SEASON OF FOOTBALL AT MILLVILLE HIGH SCHOOL.

Mike watches the action on the field as he waits on deck.

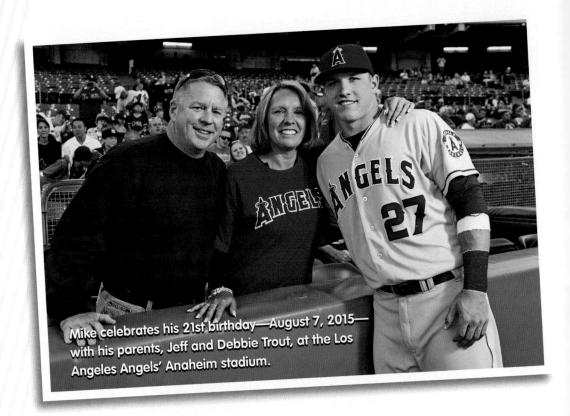

Mike celebrates his 21st birthday—August 7, 2015—with his parents, Jeff and Debbie Trout, at the Los Angeles Angels' Anaheim stadium.

tapped by the Minnesota Twins and played three seasons for their **minor league** teams. At first, it seemed like a major league career could be a possibility. However, it didn't work out that way. Jeff suffered several injuries while playing ball. In addition, he and Debbie wanted to get married. Jeff decided to hang up his baseball glove and start a family. "I didn't see myself battling through it, being a minor leaguer for another two or three years before I got a shot at the big leagues," he told grantland .com. "I thought I could hit big league pitching for sure, but it just didn't work out that way."

Giving up baseball was disappointing, but Jeff knew the game would always be part of his life. He and Debbie got married and settled down in the small New Jersey town of Vineland. Over the next five years, they added their three children to the family. When Mike was in elementary school, the Trouts moved to Millville, New Jersey.

It didn't take long for Mike to start following in his father's footsteps. "From the time he was a baby, he always would have a ball in his hand, any kind of ball," Debbie told sportsonearth .com. "He was fascinated." Mike started playing Wiffle ball when he was just a toddler. When he was five years old, he moved on to T-ball. Two years later, he started playing Little

A +
Mike also was a star in the classroom— he was in the National Honor Society.

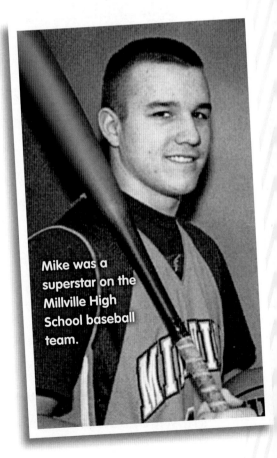

Mike was a superstar on the Millville High School baseball team.

The ultimate athlete, Mike also played basketball at Millville.

Triple Threat
Mike played baseball, basketball . . . and football at Millville!

League baseball. When he wasn't playing league games, Mike was in the backyard playing on the Trouts' homemade baseball diamond. Even then, he was a star. "Mikey used to beat us all the time," sister Teal told TheDailyJournal.com. "We wouldn't even try to get him out. He was always the best hitter, and always the fastest."

Mike loved watching his dad coach Millville High School's baseball games. At home, Jeff shared his baseball knowledge with his son. "Every chance he got, he would throw to me," Mike told insider.espn.go.com. "I'd have my buddies over and he'd be out there playing with us."

Once Mike was old enough to attend Millville High School, he was excited to join the school's baseball team. He was so good that he made the **varsity** team when he was just a freshman. For the first three years of high school, Mike was a pitcher. His abilities blew everyone away. He helped Millville win many games and racked up a huge number of RBIs and home runs.

Mike made a big change during his senior year at Millville. The team's coach decided

Number 27 poses for some fan selfies at Angel Stadium!

Senior prom night for Mike and his date!

that Mike's speed would be put to best use by moving him from the pitcher's mound to center field. It was a good move. That season Mike exploded with 18 home runs, 49 runs scored, and 45 RBIs.

"We never thought much about [Mike] playing pro baseball until his senior year when it all started to get serious," Debbie told sportsonearth.com. "Jeff and I, we're educators. We thought he'd go to college, then, maybe if everything went well. "

The major league **scouts** had other ideas. They had been watching Mike play since his sophomore year! By his senior year, the buzz around him was huge. Scouts from the New York Yankees and the Los Angeles Angels of Anaheim were particularly interested. However, Mike had college in mind. He had decided to attend East Carolina University in

Speedy

As a pitcher, Mike was able to throw as fast as 91 miles per hour (146.5 kilometers per hour).

Greenville, North Carolina. He planned to play for the school's baseball team. However, he eventually changed his mind and decided to participate in the 2009 Major League Baseball (MLB) **draft**. It was held at the MLB Network in Secaucus, New Jersey. It wasn't far from his home, so Mike and his parents went. Mike was the only player who actually was there for the draft! He wasn't picked first or second. Not even third.

Jeff paced back and forth—not worried but a bit anxious which team would pick his son.

Slide! Slide! Another base for Mike!

Mike's name wasn't called till number 25. With the cameras aimed directly at him it was obvious that he was happy . . . and just a little bit relieved.

His team? The Los Angeles Angels of Anaheim. When the MLB Network representative asked Mike his reaction, he said, "I can't wait to get out there and play ball." Then he showed off his brand-new official Los Angeles Angels cap. Jeff was as excited as his son. "We couldn't be more pleased," he told CBSsports .com. "The Angels are a solid, winning organization."

FACT FILE

THE BASICS

B-Day Fun
On Mike's 12th birthday, his dad took him to a Yankees game.

FULL NAME: Michael Nelson Trout

NICKNAMES: Mike, Mikey, Millville Meteor

BIRTHDAY: August 7, 1991

BIRTHPLACE: Vineland, New Jersey

PARENTS: Jeff and Debbie Trout

SIBLINGS: Teal and Tyler

FIRST CAR HE PLANNED TO BUY WITH BASEBALL MONEY: Toyota Tacoma

ROLE MODEL: Derek Jeter

FUN FACT: As a rookie prank, Mike had to dress up as Lady Gaga and sign autographs

TWITTER: @MikeTrout

Millville's population is about 28,000.

Because Mike was the only draftee present at the ceremony, all eyes were on him. And everyone wanted to hear what he had to say. According to www.nj.com/hssports, Mike's response was "Words can't describe that day!"

A week after the draft, on June 16, 2009, Mike reached another life milestone. He graduated high school—a sports all-star, an honor student, a millionaire! At age 18 his dreams had come true!

FACT FILE

FAVORITES

Aww!
Mike always wore his Little League uniform to bed the night before a game.

SCHOOL SUBJECT: History

TEAM SPORTS: Baseball, football, and basketball

OUTDOOR SPORTS: Fishing and hunting

INDOOR SPORT: Bowling

FOOTBALL TEAM: Philadelphia Eagles

BASKETBALL TEAM: Philadelphia 76ers

WAYS TO RELAX: Playing golf or going fishing

CAR: Custom 2015 Mercedes AMG

MUSIC: Country

HOLIDAY: Christmas

RESTAURANT: Jim's Lunch in Millville, New Jersey

BOARD GAMES: Monopoly and Scrabble

VIDEO GAME: MLB: The Show

TV SHOW: SportsCenter

"FISHING HELPS ME RELAX. MY BUDDIES AND I JUST CATCH AND RELEASE THEM."

As a minor league player for the Rancho Cucamonga Quakes, Mike made a good reputation for himself!

BE LIKE MIKE . . .
TROUT

A DIAMOND ON THE DIAMOND!

June 2009 . . . the draft was over and Mike had his Angels cap, but he wasn't headed straight to Anaheim. In pro baseball, players have to work their way up to the big leagues. They start by playing on minor league teams that work together with the major league teams. Mike started the 2009 season with the AZL Angels and finished it playing with the Cedar Rapids Kernels. In 2010, still with the Kernels, his performance earned him a spot in the All-Star Futures Game. After that game, he was named the second-best overall minor league player. This led to a place on the Rancho Cucamonga Quakes. At the end of the season, he won the Topps Minor League Player of the Year award.

MORE THAN 800,000 FANS FOLLOW MIKE ON TWITTER.

Mike started the 2011 season with the Arkansas Travelers, but his minor league career was rapidly drawing to a close. On July 8, he made his major league debut with the Los Angeles Angels of Anaheim. Unfortunately, it was not Mike's best game. He didn't get a single hit! His next game went a little better, and he scored an infield hit against the Seattle Mariners.

At this point, Mike started really racking up the frequent-flier miles. He was sent down to the Arkansas Travelers on August 1 and then sent back up to Anaheim on August 19. That night, he hit his first major league home run at Angel Stadium. He finished the season back with the Travelers, but he began the 2012 season with the Salt Lake Bees.

The Trout family had gotten used to Mike's moves from team to team, but they had their fingers crossed that 2012 would be the year he would finally win a more permanent position

DAD 😊

Jeff never misses one of Mike's games. He's there in person or watches on TV!

Mike's Timeline

The Millville Meteor's Journey

2009
Mike is named New Jersey Gatorade Baseball Player of the Year

JUNE 9, 2009
Mike is chosen by the Los Angeles Angels of Anaheim

as the 25th overall pick in the MLB draft

2009
Mike plays with the Angels' minor league teams, the AZL Angels and the Cedar Rapids Kernels

with the Angels. Debbie recalled those anxious days to sportsonearth .com: "September 1 is when the **rosters** are expanded. We figured that was the way it was. We figured Mike would spend the summer in Salt Lake City, . . . learn a lot. Then get a chance to taste the big leagues in September.

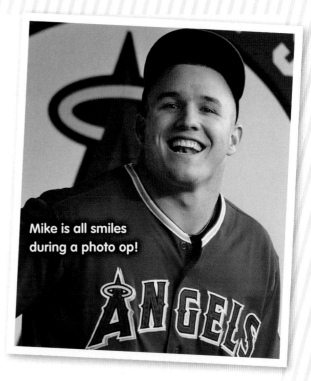

Mike is all smiles during a photo op!

. . . When he didn't make the team in spring training, we figured that was the way it was. You know, though, we went out to visit him in Salt Lake City and he had a look about him that I never had seen before. He was on a mission. That's the only way I explain it. He was very serious in a way I never had seen. On a mission."

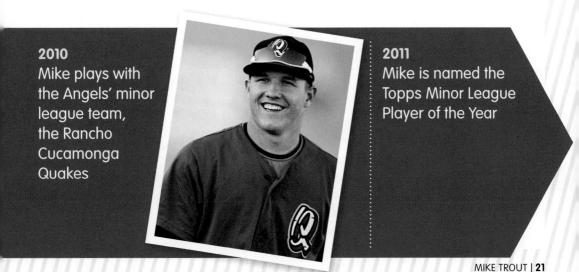

2010
Mike plays with the Angels' minor league team, the Rancho Cucamonga Quakes

2011
Mike is named the Topps Minor League Player of the Year

Mission accomplished. On April 28, Mike was brought back up to Anaheim to join the team's starting lineup. During May and June, he broke records and scored runs left and right. He was even picked to play in the July 2012 All-Star Game. It was a great year for Mike—he was the first MLB player in history to hit 30 home runs, steal 45 bases, and score 125 runs in one season. The only disappointment was coming in second behind Miguel Cabrera for the 2012 American League Most Valuable Player (MVP) award. In his 2013 season, Mike hit his very first grand slam. He also scored his 200th career run. He played in the All-Star Game again. And once again, he was in the running for the 2013 American League MVP award, but again he came in second to Miguel Cabrera.

FAMILY

In 2015, the Angels drafted Aaron Cox, the little bro of Mike's girlfriend!

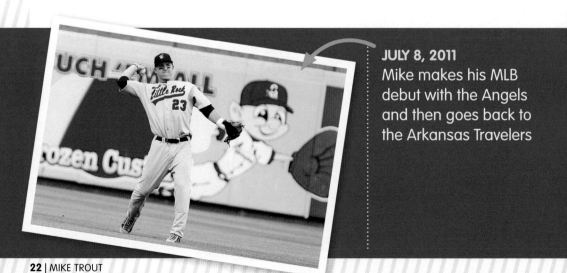

JULY 8, 2011
Mike makes his MLB debut with the Angels and then goes back to the Arkansas Travelers

Happy days! Mike helped the Angels clinch the American League Western Division title in 2014.

In the 2014 season, Mike made his third appearance in the All-Star Game. This time, he was named the game's MVP. He also finally won the American League MVP award. In 2015, Mike continued his meteoric career. He reached the milestone of 100 career home runs and 100 career stolen bases on April 17, 2015. When July 2015

JULY 24, 2011
Mike hits his first major league home run in a game against the Baltimore Orioles

2011
Mike is named Baseball America Minor League Player of the Year

APRIL 28, 2012
Mike joins the Angels' starting lineup

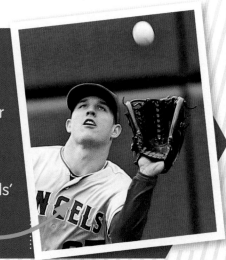

Not only did Mike meet his idol, Derek Jeter, but he played with him in the 2014 All-Star Game.

rolled around, Mike was once again on the winning AL All-Star team. He hit two home runs and made history by being the first player named All-Star MVP back-to-back.

Competitors cheer when Mike makes a big play or breaks a record. He has become one of MLB's biggest stars!

JULY 10, 2012
Mike plays in his first MLB All-Star Game

NOVEMBER 20, 2012
Mike wins the MLB Rookie of the Year award

JULY 16, 2013
Mike plays in his second MLB All-Star Game

JULY 15, 2014
Mike plays in his third MLB All-Star Game

Even before he was wowing sports fans in 2015, Mike made his family proud when he appeared on the cover of the August 27, 2012, issue of *Sports Illustrated*. "It's every athlete's dream to be on the cover of *Sports Illustrated*," his dad told nj.com. "We are proud of him and humbled by it. It's a tremendous thing for a kid from Millville and Cumberland County to be on the cover of *Sports Illustrated*. It's the premier sports magazine in the country."

If Mike's parents were happy about their son's success, the people of Millville were over the moon! Ever since Mike had been playing for Millville teams, he had won the town's heart. And when success came Mike's way, he didn't forget where he came from. As a matter of fact,

Twitter Love

Mike gets about one marriage proposal every hour on Twitter.

NOVEMBER 13, 2014
Mike is named the American League MVP

JULY 14, 2015
Mike plays in his fourth MLB All-Star game. The AL wins, and Mike is named MVP for the second year in a row

even though he is a pro athlete, he still lives at home with his parents during the off-season! "A lot of my teammates make fun of me because I still live with my parents," he told espn.go.com. "Eventually I'll get a house. But I'm real close to my parents."

Mike is close to the whole town of Millville. When he's back in town, you constantly hear people saying, "Hi, Mike!" or "Way to go, Mike!" In some ways, his success is the town's success. The people of Millville know that

> "I WANT TO PLAY PRO BALL; THAT'S BEEN MY DREAM."

when Mike's home, he's just a regular guy. You can still see him down at Jim's Lunch, placing his usual order of six hamburgers "with just sauce." As a matter of fact, when Mike was home right before the May 2014 game against the Phillies, which was dubbed Millville Night, a local gas station flew a banner that said, "Hey Mike Trout! Hit a homer at Millville Night and I'll buy you and ten Millville locals six Jim's burgers 'with just sauce.'"

Mike doesn't bask in the praise. He gives back to the people who have supported him throughout his career. He has sponsored the Millville Angels, which is a traveling baseball team for kids 10 years old and younger. He has also sponsored a local kids' basketball team. As a surprise Mike had gifts for the entire Millville Thunderbolts baseball team. When the players came into the gym and saw a Christmas tree with orange boxes underneath, they started high-fiving. There was a pair of Mike's Nike Lunar Vapor Trout model cleats for each one of them. With the shoes was a card that said, "Your future gets brighter today! Go and make your mark on Thunderbolt baseball and have a great season."

Mike also teamed up with the BodyArmor sports drink to donate $20,000 to Millville High School for the baseball facilities. And these gifts are just the ones that have made the newspapers. Mike loves being part of the Millville family and no matter where the future takes him, his heart will always be there.

Along with the Thunderbolt's team and coaches Mike dedicates the Mike Trout Field at Millville High School in 2014.

Mike has gotten
used to chatting
with the press.

MIKE TALKS BASEBALL . . . AND MORE

HE PROVES HE'S JUST A BOY NEXT DOOR

Mike Trout has been playing baseball almost since he could walk. When he first threw a baseball, he knew exactly what he wanted to do for the rest of his life. He was drafted by the Los Angeles Angels of Anaheim in 2009 and won the Rookie of the Year award in 2012. He continually racks up new records and awards. His fan base is in the millions. And though he is somewhat shy, he loves talking about baseball . . . and his family, his hometown, and his fans. Read on!

On the first time he played in Philadelphia as an Angel . . . "It [meant] a lot, you know, playing in front of all your hometown fans. You know, the ovation, yeah, I was surprised. I knew I was going to get some cheers. I thought I was going to get booed. You never

Mike hit a triple against his "hometown" team, the Philadelphia Phillies.

know. I've been to Phillies games and I've been to a lot of Eagles games and I know if you're wearing somebody else's jersey in their stadium, you're going to get booed. So, yeah, I thought [the cheers] were cool. It means a lot for sure."

STAR!
Mike holds records both in home runs and bases stolen!

On the Mike Trout Field in his hometown, Millville, New Jersey . . . "For me, being able to give back is something special and an honor . . . it's very important to me. And then having them all here today for this just makes the whole thing even better."

On the best tease about his last name . . .

"When I was in Toronto . . . I was in left field and everybody in left field—or maybe it was the whole stadium—was chanting 'Here fishy, fishy, fishy!' That was pretty intense but also pretty cool. And funny, actually."

On the worst name tease . . . "Signs like, 'You smell like fish.' I mean, c'mon."

Mike poses after batting practice for his first MLB game at Baltimore.

On the nickname "Millville Meteor" . . . "I was [at a] signing a couple of weeks ago and people were like, 'I have to get this on the ball.' And I talked to a guy, and I guess someone went on Wikipedia under my name—you know how anyone can edit it?—and someone put that on my Wikipedia page. And ever since that, it's been my nickname. I [had been] wondering the same thing: Who came up with it and what is it?"

On being scouted by the New York Yankees while he was in high school . . . "I got to know the Yankees scouts a little bit. I introduced myself. They would just show up at random games. It was pretty crazy."

Mike greets fans and friends at a Phillies game.

On his talent for stealing bases . . . "Just being aggressive—that's the way I think of it. Knowing what you're doing before the play happens. If I'm on first base, I want to steal second. So, you know, even when I'm on first and don't steal second? Base hit anywhere. I want to

It's a steal! It's a steal! Mike loves it!

be on third. Lots of big innings start when you go first to third. Just being aggressive and knowing what you're doing."

On leaping higher than the Baltimore Orioles' center field fence to stop J. J. Hardy's home run . . . "That one was probably the first thing in the majors where I felt fired up on a different level. It was

No homer this day for J. J. Hardy! Mike snags the ball!

just . . . different. When it came off the bat, I didn't think it was going to be a home run at first, and then I got to the track. I jumped, I came down, I looked at Torii [Hunter, the Angels' outfielder], and he said, 'Look in your glove!' I didn't realize it."

On his batting practice methods . . . "There's always things you can do in the cages, like the high ball on the tee. The other thing is first just trying to get on top of the baseball, and I think the biggest thing is just swinging at strikes. Getting up and down, and swinging at strikes and a majority of them are falling off in the zone or off the plate high, so it's getting my pitch and just hitting it and not trying to do too much."

On his parents' support of his baseball dreams . . . "They always told me that if they had to put a uniform on me, they didn't want to do it. Baseball was a thing where I woke up every day ready to play. It's always been fun. I was probably driving them crazy to play."

"IF I'M NOT 30 MINUTES EARLY, I FEEL LIKE I'M LATE."

On his first major league game . . . "First at-bat, I lined out to third. The second at-bat, I lined out to right field . . . It was just one of those games."

Mike meets his giant bobblehead at a game with the Texas Rangers.

MIKE TROUT'S SCOREBOARD

TAKE A PEEK AT MIKE'S FAVE FOODS, FUN FACTS, AND LIFE ON AND OFF THE FIELD!

FUN-TASTIC FACTS

- Mike would rather hit 40 homers than steal 60 bases.
- Mike attended the 2008 World Series when the Phillies won—but he wasn't in the stadium. He was tailgating with his friends because they couldn't get tickets!
- Mike's Christmas presents are still signed "From Santa," thanks to his mom!
- Mike planned to be a history teacher like his dad if he didn't make it in MLB.

FOOD FEST

REGULAR ORDER AT JIM'S LUNCH
SIX HAMBURGERS
WITH JIM'S SECRET SAUCE

SPORTS DRINK
MIKE DRINKS BODYARMOR—"I CRAMP UP A LOT, SO DRINKING IT BEFORE THE GAME AND DURING IT HELPS ME HYDRATE."

SNACKS
CHIPS

CANDY
SWEDISH FISH AND SOUR PATCH KIDS

PIZZA PARLOR
S&J PIZZERIA IN MILLVILLE

DINNER
SALTED BONE-IN STEAKS

SIDE DISH
TEAMMATE LUIS JIMENEZ'S DOMINICAN RICE

"GROWING UP, I WAS SUCH A PICKY EATER. I'M FINALLY STARTING TO EXPAND."

MIKE'S MAN CAVE

Even after going to the "Bigs," Mike has continued living at his parents' house. It's comfortable. He has taken over the basement and turned it into his special getaway.

- A Ping-Pong table (he's very, very good!)
- A dartboard
- A bar stocked with BodyArmor sports drinks
- An Xbox
- A Fathead poster of himself on the wall
- Remote-controlled cars and airplanes
- The baseball wall—autographed baseballs Mike has collected over the years, including Derek Jeter, Albert Pujols and Mariano Rivera. "Then, up there, is a big one I got this year: my Mickey Mantle ball."

Mickey Mantle

WEATHER GEEK

"I would love to try it," Mike once revealed about being a TV weatherman. Here are some of Mike's weather quirks!

- He has a folder on his smartphone with only weather apps.
- The Angels always check out the day's weather with Mike.
- Mike retweets forecasts and posts them on Facebook.
- He's hoping for a one-day gig on the Weather Channel during the off-season.
- His interest in weather started with snow days during school.

BASEBALL TERMS

ACE: A team's best pitcher

BAG: A base

BULL PEN: An area where relief pitchers can warm up before entering the game

CURVEBALL: A pitch that curves to the left when thrown with the right hand or to the right when thrown with the left hand

DUGOUT: The area where coaches and players hang out when they aren't on the field

FASTBALL: A pitch that heads straight toward the plate at top speed

GRAND SLAM: A home run that is hit while players are on all three bases; this gives a team four runs at once

MOUND: The hill a pitcher throws from

RELIEF PITCHER: A replacement for the starting pitcher

STRIKE ZONE: The area over home plate the ball must pass through to qualify as a strike

WHIFF: To strike out

YAKKER: Curveball

MIKE'S TEAMS AND POSITIONS

LITTLE LEAGUE
Position: Shortstop

Jersey: #2 in honor of Derek Jeter

SUMMER TRAVELING LEAGUE
Team: Tri-State Arsenal

Position: Pitcher

MILLVILLE HIGH SCHOOL
Team: Thunderbolts

Positions: Pitcher, center field

Jersey: #1

MLB ROOKIE LEAGUE
Teams: AZL Angels, Cedar Rapids Kernels (2009–2010)

Position: Center field

MLB CLASS A
Team: Rancho Cucamonga Quakes (2010)

Position: Center field

MLB DOUBLE-A
Team: Arkansas Travelers (2011)

Position: Center field

MLB TRIPLE-A
Team: Salt Lake Bees (2012)

Position: Center field

MAJOR LEAGUE BASEBALL
Team: Los Angeles Angels of Anaheim (2012–present)

Position: Center field

Jersey: #27

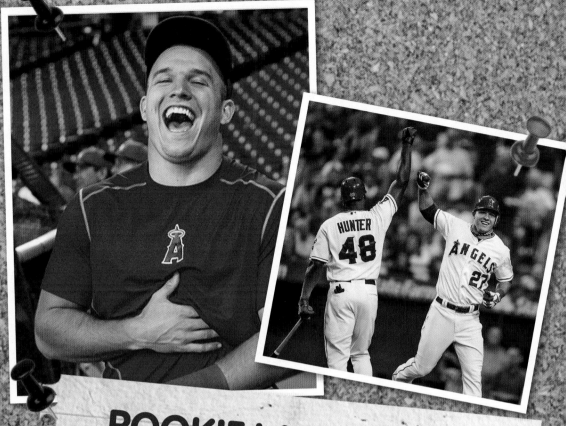

ROOKIE LAUGHS

A player's first year is spent trying to excel on the field and fit in with the team. Sometimes it includes pranks pulled by the older players. Mike faced a few good ones, but one prank he will never forget is when outfielder Torii Hunter told Mike he would race him for $100. Mike said, "Let's go," thinking he could definitely beat Torii. Torii then pointed out that it didn't matter who won the race. He had said only that he would race Mike for $100, not that he would win!

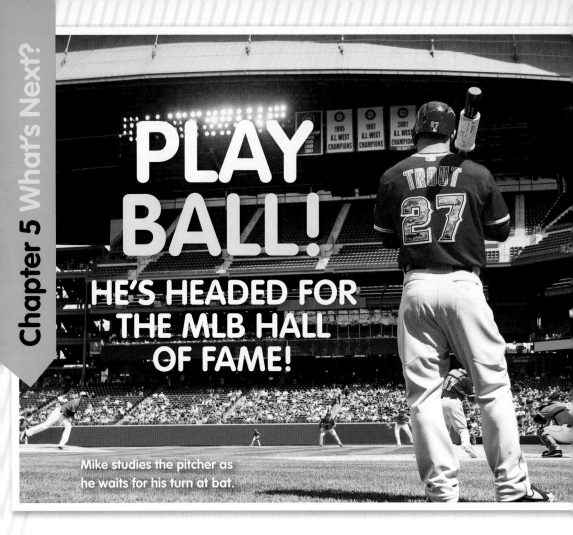

PLAY BALL!

HE'S HEADED FOR THE MLB HALL OF FAME!

Mike studies the pitcher as he waits for his turn at bat.

"What's nice about it is Mike is such a good person," Millville's radio broadcaster and former mayor Jim Quinn said to CSNPhilly .com. "You get some of these superstar athletes that have attitudes and aren't really genuine, but Mike is a genuinely nice guy. You see him signing autographs as he's walking down the left-field line. It's wonderful that such a good thing happens to such a good person."

That's the general feeling about Mike—he's a superstar, yet still humble and down-to-earth. As for his talent, former MLB commissioner Bud Selig

A SIGN ON THE ROAD LEADING INTO MIKE'S HOMETOWN READS "WELCOME TO MILLVILLE, HOME OF MIKE TROUT."

recalled discussing Mike's abilities with a scout. "I said, 'Compare him to somebody,'" Selig's conversation was reported on espn.go.com. "He thought for a second—and he was dead serious—and he said, 'Mickey Mantle–type ability.' And that's breathtaking. Really breathtaking. Mickey Mantle–type ability."

If the former commissioner feels that way about Mike, imagine what his teammates think. "I think it's fair to say he's well on his way to being one of the greatest ever," Angels third baseman David Freese told espn.go.com. Dave Hansen, an Angels hitting coach added, "In 20–25 years, I think we'll be saying, 'That was probably one of the best athletes we've ever seen in the modern era.' We'll say, 'He was amazing. He could hit. He could run like you wouldn't believe. And

Mike is always smiling! Why not? He's happy!

AFTER MIKE MADE A DONATION TO MILLVILLE HIGH SCHOOL'S BASEBALL FIELD, THE SCHOOL NAMED IT AFTER HIM!

how 'bout his baseball instincts?' That's what we're going to be saying. And just his numbers. Look at his numbers. I mean, they compare with all the greats."

Being compared to the greats of baseball isn't Mike's favorite thing. He'd rather watch them—live on the field or on video—and learn. "I'm not one of those guys who says, I want to be like this guy or be like that, with those kinds of numbers," Mike told espn.go.com. Though he is still young, Mike has learned that understanding his talent, improving his skills, and not trying to imitate anyone else is the way to go.

Of course, there are still players Mike looks up to. One of them, of course, is Derek Jeter. "He has always been my favorite player to watch, just the way he carried himself on and off the field, winning championships," Mike revealed to *USA Today*.

Right now, Mike's personal goal is to help win championships for his team. Many baseball experts think Mike is going to meet that goal again and again. However, that's not the only thing he cares about. Coach Hansen explained to espn.go.com, "This kid is on the road to greatness, I think. He's that special. But if there's a little kid around, if there's somebody that wants to meet him, he engages that. He takes the time. And that's the kind of person that I'm looking at, more than the baseball player. He's a well-raised young man. Mike Trout loves—I mean loves—the competition. But if there's a moment where he can show some humility and some compassion for a young kid, he's going to do it. I've seen it already. That's pretty special, I think."

Mike thinks his life is pretty special, too, and he's determined to work hard to keep growing and setting goals for himself!

MLB
"It's everything I thought it would be."

The whole team congratulates Mike when he returns to the Angels dugout!

Resources

BOOKS

Fishman, Jon M. *Mike Trout*. Minneapolis: Lerner Publications, 2014.

Gagne, Tammy. *Mike Trout*. Hockessin, DE: Mitchell Lane Publishers, 2014.

ARTICLE

Sports Illustrated, May 12, 2014
"The Best Beyond a Shadow of a Trout."

Facts for Now

Visit this Scholastic Web site for more information on **Mike Trout**: www.factsfornow.scholastic.com Enter the keywords **Mike Trout**

Glossary

draft *(DRAFT)* a process that pro sports teams use to select new players from high school or college teams

minor league *(MYE-nur LEEG)* professional baseball league where players prepare for Major League Baseball

RBIs *(ARE BEE EYZ)* a measurement of runs scored while a player is at bat in baseball; short for "runs batted in"

rosters *(RAH-sturz)* lists of players on a sports team

scouts *(SKOUTS)* representatives from professional teams who observe young athletes to see if they are good enough to play pro sports

varsity *(VAR-suh-tee)* the main sports team of a school, consisting of its best players

Index

Acknowledgments

Page 8: Jeff on Minor Leagues: grantland.com May 14, 2015
Page 9: Debbie on baby mike: sportsonearth.com August 29, 2012
Page 10: Teal on Mike: TheDailyJournal.com
Page 10: Mike playing ball with Jeff: insider.espn.go.com June 15, 2014
Page 12: Debbie on Mike going to college: sportsonearth.com August 29, 2012
Page 14: Mike on Angels draft: sportsonearth.com August 29, 2012
Page 14: Jeff on draft: CBSsports.com June 9, 2009
Page 16: Mike's response to draft: nj.com/hssports June 9, 2009
Page 17: Fishing: espn.go.com 2009
Page 21: Debbie on Salt Lake City: sportsonearth.com August 29, 2012

Page 25: *Sports Illustrated*: nj.com/Cumberland May 11, 2014
Page 26: Living with parents: insider.espn.go.com June 15, 2014
Page 26: Banner: nj.com/Cumberland May 11, 2014
Page 26: Pro Ball: espn .go.com June 5, 2009
Page 27: Thunderbolts Christmas gifts: Thedailyjournal.com March 26, 2015
Page 29: On playing Phillies: MLB Network *Intentional Talk* interview June 17, 2014
Page 30: On Mike Trout Field: MLB Network *Intentional Talk* interview June 17, 2014
Page 31: On best tease: sport s.yahoo.com December 24, 2012
Page 31: On worst tease: sports.yahoo.com December 24, 2012

Page 32: On "Millville Meteor": sports.yahoo.com December 24, 2012
Page 32: On NY Yankees scouts: gq.com September 2012
Page 32: On stealing bases: gq.com September 2012
Page 33: On Baltimore Oriole's homerun-stopping leap: *GQ* March 2013
Page 34: On batting practice: haloheaven.com June 2, 2015
Page 34: On parents' support: insider.espn.go.com June 15, 2014
Page 35: First major league at-bat: espn.go.com September 20, 2012
Page 35: Being early: espn .go.com September 20, 2012
Page 37: BodyArmour: sports .yahoo.com September 21, 2012
Page 37: Picky eater: BrainyQuote.com

Page 38: Mickey Mantle ball: *GQ* March 2013
Page 38: Being a weatherman: sports.yahoo.com August 19, 2015
Page 39: Baseball Terms: Epicsports.com
Page 41: Rookie Laughs: Pressofatlanticcity.com July 1, 2012
Page 42: Jim Quinn quote: NBC Sports/CSNPhilly.com May 13, 2014
Page 43: Bud Selig quote: espn.go.com July 15, 2014
Page 43: David Freese/Dave Hansen quote: espn.go.com July 15, 2014
Page 44: Comparisons: espn .go.com July 15, 2014
Page 44: On Derek Jeter: *USA Today* February 20, 2014
Page 44: Dave Hansen: espn .go.com July 15, 2014
Page 45: MLB: *NY Times* June 23, 2012

About the Author

Marie Morreale is the author of many official and unofficial celebrity biographies. She attended New York University as an English/creative writing major and began her writing and editorial career in New York City. As the editor of teen/music magazines *Teen Machine* and *Jam!*, she covered TV, film, and music personalities and interviewed superstars such as Michael Jackson, Britney Spears, and Justin Timberlake/*NSYNC. Morreale was also an editor/writer at Little Golden Books.

Today, she is the executive editor, media, of Scholastic classroom magazines writing about pop culture, sports, news, and special events. Morreale lives in New York City and is entertained daily by her two Maine coon cats, Cher and Sullivan.